SO-EIL-098

Taking EARTH'S Temperature

TURNING UP THE HEAT

Tara Haelle

rourkeeducationalmedia.com

Before & After Reading Activities

Before Reading:

Building Academic Vocabulary and Background Knowledge

Before reading a book, it is important to tap into what your child or students already know about the topic. This will help them develop their vocabulary, increase their reading comprehension, and make connections across the curriculum.

1. Look at the cover of the book. What will this book be about?
2. What do you already know about the topic?
3. Let's study the Table of Contents. What will you learn about in the book's chapters?
4. What would you like to learn about this topic? Do you think you might learn about it from this book? Why or why not?
5. Use a reading journal to write about your knowledge of this topic. Record what you already know about the topic and what you hope to learn about the topic.
6. Read the book.
7. In your reading journal, record what you learned about the topic and your response to the book.
8. After reading the book complete the activities below.

Content Area Vocabulary

Read the list. What do these words mean?

atmosphere

climate

deforestation

droughts

ecosystem

fossil fuels

glaciers

greenhouse gases

heat wave

hurricanes

After Reading:

Comprehension and Extension Activity

After reading the book, work on the following questions with your child or students in order to check their level of reading comprehension and content mastery.

1. What are some examples of climate change? (Summarize)
2. Why is it difficult to predict exactly what the effects of climate change will be? (Infer)
3. What is an example of common human activity that produces greenhouse gases? (Asking Questions)
4. What is one climate change effect that you personally have experienced? (Text to Self Connection)
5. What are some ways that rising sea levels might directly affect people? (Asking Questions)

Extension Activity

What is a weather-related disaster you have heard about recently in the news or from friends or family? Describe how that storm formed or the disaster occurred. What were the natural causes of the disaster? Did any human behaviors or activities contribute to the formation of the disaster? Make a list of things people can do to be prepared if a similar disaster happens to them and what, if anything, people can do to make those disasters less likely.

TABLE OF CONTENTS

CHAPTER ONE

UNDERSTANDING CLIMATE

Step outside and feel the air. Is it hot? Cold? Warm? Wet or windy? The weather changes day to day because of local changes in the **atmosphere**, the layer of gases surrounding Earth. But there are reliable patterns to the weather, such as more frequent thunderstorms in spring.

Weather patterns in one place over time make up a region's **climate**. Climate includes average temperatures, precipitation, wind patterns, humidity, and storms over decades or centuries.

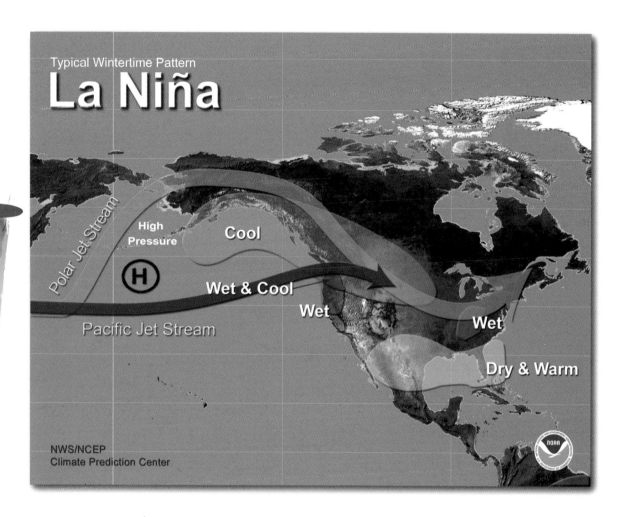

Typical Wintertime Pattern

La Niña

Polar Jet Stream

High Pressure

Cool

(H)

Wet & Cool

Wet

Pacific Jet Stream

Wet

Dry & Warm

NWS/NCEP
Climate Prediction Center

SEA CIRCULATION

Earth's oceans have an especially big influence on climate. They absorb the sun's energy and distribute its heat throughout the atmosphere. Ocean currents also carry warm water from the equator to the North and South Poles and bring cold water back. This circulation of warm and cold currents keeps climates stable.

The Sahara Desert's climate is hot and dry. In tropical countries, such as Vietnam, the climate is hot and humid. Mountain climates are often humid and cold. In the United States, the climate in a southern state like Texas is much warmer throughout the year than in a northern state like Pennsylvania.

The Sahara Desert, Africa

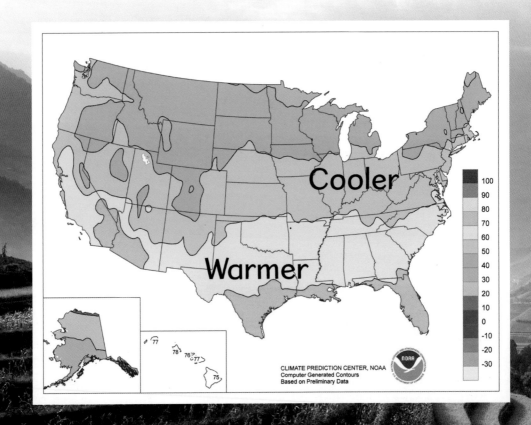

Sulfur dioxide

WHEN HOT MAKES COLD

Volcanic eruptions might be hot, but they can cause the climate to cool. Eruptions release a gas called sulfur dioxide. In the atmosphere, the gas becomes small particles that reflect sunlight away from the Earth. Less light means less warmth.

Climate changes over hundreds and thousands of years. Natural events cause much of this change. Ocean currents, rainfall patterns, volcanic eruptions, sun storms, sun spots, and shifts in Earth's orbit all affect climate.

The global climate also goes through historical cycles, warming and cooling over thousands of years.

Greenland

NORTH AMERICA

THE LITTLE ICE AGE

The Little Ice Age, starting around the 14th to 16th centuries and lasting through the late 19th century, demonstrates natural climate variations. Scientists are unsure what caused it. Some scientists think less sun radiation caused the cooler temperatures. Others attribute it to multiple volcanic eruptions between 1275 and 1300 CE.

September 1986

Late Summer 1917

The Athabasca Glacier, located in the Canadian Rockies, is shrinking at a rate of 16 feet (5 meters) per year. It has receded nearly a mile (1.6 kilometers) in the past 125 years.

For example, **glaciers**, huge chunks of moving ice, have grown and shrunk seven times in the past 750,000 years, according to the National Aeronautics and Space Administration (NASA). But human activity causes changes in climate too.

CHAPTER TWO

HOW HUMANS AFFECT CLIMATE CHANGE

Humans' biggest influence on climate is increasing **greenhouse gases** in the atmosphere. Greenhouse gases are chemicals that trap the sun's heat in the atmosphere just as a greenhouse does to keep plants warm.

Car exhaust from burning fuel contains greenhouse gases.

The more greenhouse gases the atmosphere contains, the warmer the planet is. The most abundant greenhouse gases are carbon dioxide, methane, and nitrous oxide.

People burn coal for energy.

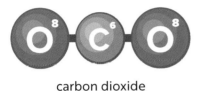

carbon dioxide

nitrous oxide

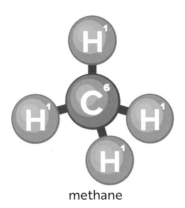

methane

THE KEELING CURVE

Scientists use a graph called the Keeling Curve to chart how much carbon dioxide is in the atmosphere. It's named for Charles David Keeling (1928 – 2005), the scientist whose measurements at the Mauna Loa Observatory in Hawaii first showed how quickly carbon dioxide levels were rising.

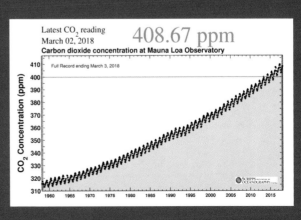

Latest CO_2 reading March 02, 2018
408.67 ppm
Carbon dioxide concentration at Mauna Loa Observatory

Full Record ending March 3, 2018

CO₂ Concentration (ppm)

SCRIPPS INSTITUTION OF OCEANOGRAPHY

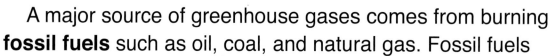

A major source of greenhouse gases comes from burning **fossil fuels** such as oil, coal, and natural gas. Fossil fuels form from dead plants and animals over millions of years.

coal

The air pollution from coal plants can also cause health problems such as asthma, cancer, and heart and lung problems.

COWS PASSING GAS

Cows produce methane—with their farts and burps! A single cow can produce anywhere from 30 to 236 gallons (114 to 893 liters) of methane daily. With about 1.5 billion cows on Earth, that's a lot of belching and farting warming up our planet. That's why cattle farming is one source of climate change.

An average airplane releases 53 pounds (24 kilograms) of carbon dioxide for every mile it flies.

The natural formation of these fuels releases methane, but burning them for energy releases billions of tons of carbon dioxide into the atmosphere each year. In fact, humans release more than 40 billion tons (36 billion metric tons) of carbon dioxide into the atmosphere every year.

Deforestation, when people cut down and burn forests for wood and farmland, is another source of carbon dioxide. Trees and other plants remove carbon dioxide from the air to make food through photosynthesis, but when a tree is cut down, it releases stored carbon dioxide.

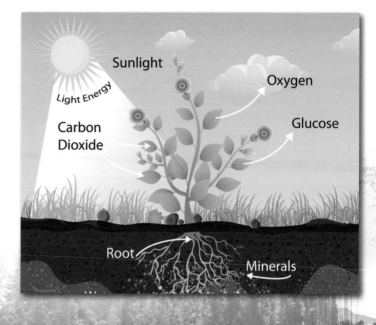

Sunlight

Light Energy

Carbon Dioxide

Oxygen

Glucose

Root

Minerals

DEFORESTATION'S CARBON FOOTPRINT

Every car or plane ride you take releases carbon dioxide into the air. But deforestation has a larger carbon footprint, the amount of carbon dioxide it contributes to the atmosphere. Deforestation adds more carbon dioxide to the air than all cars and trucks on the world's roads combined.

Human activities also produce methane, which traps 30 times more heat than carbon dioxide. Farming, raising livestock, and the decomposing waste in landfills all release methane.

Trapping Heat on Earth

Methane

Carbon Dioxide

One pound of Methane can trap the same amount of heat as 16 pounds of Carbon Dioxide

Landfills make up the third largest source of methane from human activities in the U.S., but capturing that methane could actually save energy.

Climate skeptics argue greenhouse gases do not affect the global climate much. They point out natural causes of climate change and climate cycles over time. They say humans have little control over such a complex system.

Smog, a type of air pollution, results from mixtures of sunlight and smoke or other chemicals in the air. Breathing in too much smog can be harmful.

But nearly all scientists insist that the amount of carbon dioxide alone that humans produce has a big effect on the world's climate.

RICE PADDY PROBLEMS

Methane in the atmosphere has begun rapidly increasing from rice agriculture. Bacteria, one-celled organisms that breathe carbon dioxide, live in rice paddies and release methane. As carbon dioxide levels climb, rice grows faster—but so do the bacteria. So the rise of one greenhouse gas is causing another to rise, too.

CHAPTER THREE

TRYING TO PREDICT THE FUTURE

Scientists compare a warming climate to drawing a bath. Just as water fills a bathtub, greenhouse gases are filling the atmosphere. A drain lets water leave the bathtub just as plants and oceans remove greenhouse gases from the atmosphere.

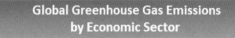

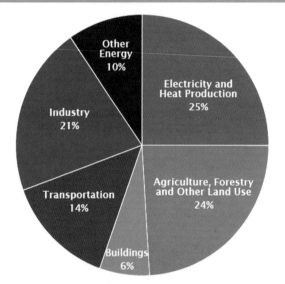

Global Greenhouse Gas Emissions by Economic Sector

- Other Energy 10%
- Electricity and Heat Production 25%
- Industry 21%
- Agriculture, Forestry and Other Land Use 24%
- Transportation 14%
- Buildings 6%

One way people can reduce greenhouse gas emissions is to carpool, use public transportation, or ride a bicycle instead of driving a car.

Greenhouse Gas Buildup

But when water flows into the tub faster than it drains, the tub slowly fills with water. Right now, greenhouse gases are entering the atmosphere faster than plants and oceans can remove them. So the atmosphere is slowly heating up.

Observed U.S. Temperature Change

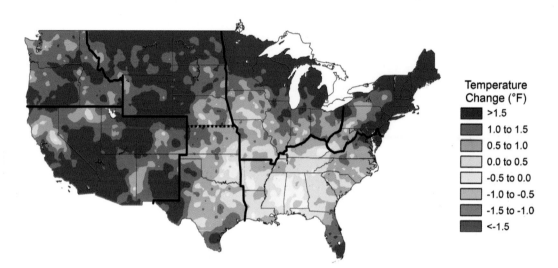

Temperature Change (°F)
- >1.5
- 1.0 to 1.5
- 0.5 to 1.0
- 0.0 to 0.5
- -0.5 to 0.0
- -1.0 to -0.5
- -1.5 to -1.0
- <-1.5

A report from the U.S. Global Change Research Program in 2017 found the world's air temperature has warmed 1.8 degrees Fahrenheit (1 degree Celsius) since 1901. Even that small change can lead to major effects. "This period is now the warmest in the history of modern civilization," the report said.

As glaciers melt faster than in the past, more water flows to the ocean and increases sea levels.

A world organization of scientists called the Intergovernmental Panel on Climate Change (IPCC) studies climate change. Climate scientists try to predict how the climate will change by examining past climate patterns. They use mathematical models based on those patterns to calculate how much Earth might warm or the seas might rise from melting ice.

SHRINKING ICE SHEETS

The IPCC discovered that large sheets of ice in the Arctic have shrunk every year since 1979 as less ice re-freezes each winter. Understanding how quickly these sheets shrink under certain conditions will help scientists predict how much more they will continue decreasing as conditions change.

Climate research is challenging since so many natural and human events are involved. Many of these events interact in **feedback loops**. In a feedback loop, one event affects another, which then affects the first event again in an ongoing cycle.

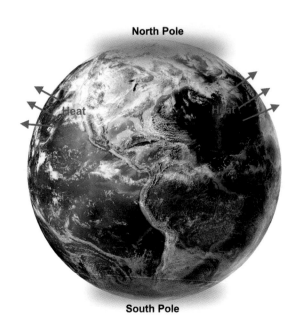

North Pole

Heat   Heat

South Pole

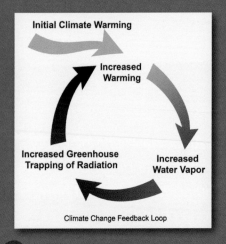

Initial Climate Warming

Increased
Warming

Increased Greenhouse
Trapping of Radiation

Increased
Water Vapor

Climate Change Feedback Loop

A FEEDBACK LOOP

Trapped heat from greenhouse gases melts glaciers and ice caps near the North and South Poles and warms the ocean. The ocean releases this heat and warms the atmosphere. The warming atmosphere melts more glaciers and ice caps. These alternating effects of melting ice and warming oceans create a feedback loop.

Architects are finding ways to build "greener" buildings that use less energy and produce less greenhouse gases.

Some people think humans will adapt to a changing climate just as they have in the past. Plants and animals that cannot adapt may go extinct, they say, but extinctions have occurred for millions of years. They do not see climate change as a problem.

But most scientists and political leaders see climate change as a threat. They warn that humans, animals, and plants will suffer dangerous consequences if they cannot keep up with how rapidly the climate is changing.

MELTING UNDER THEIR FEET

Dwindling ice in the North and South Poles endangers wildlife there. Polar bears and walruses in the North Pole and penguins in the South Pole need ice for hunting, traveling, breeding, and raising their young. Walrus calves wait on sea ice while mothers hunt, but melting ice sometimes leaves them unprotected in the water.

MAKING PREDICTIONS

When scientists make predictions about climate change, they use data from past events they have observed and measured. But there will always be factors they do not know about or cannot measure that will affect future events. In this activity, let's see how well you can use past events to predict future ones.

YOU'LL NEED:

- Any type of ball
- Note paper
- Pen or pencil
- A slide in the park, playground, or backyard
- One sticker (any kind)
- 15 bottle caps, coasters, sticky notes or other objects you can use to mark a location on the ground (You will need three different sets of five markers, example: 5 bottle caps, 5 sticky notes, and 5 coasters.)

DIRECTIONS:

1. Climb to the top of the slide and place the sticker at the very top of the slope. This is the place where you will roll the ball down the slide.

2. Place the ball squarely on the sticker and gently let go, trying not to bump the ball in any particular direction.

3. Climb down and wait for the ball to land and stop rolling. Mark the spot with a bottle cap, coaster, or other item that can be later removed.

4. Repeat steps 2 and 3 four more times.

5. After you have at least five markers for the ball's landing each time, make some guesses about where the ball will land next based on where it landed the first five times. Pick five locations and put down the other set of markers where you think the ball will land.

6. Repeat steps 2 and 3 five times. Use the third type of marker to mark where the ball actually lands on each roll.

7. Compare your predictions to where the ball landed on the second set of rolls. How accurate were your predictions? How did the ball's landing places compare to the first set of rolls? What different factors might have affected where the ball landed each time?

8. Try the experiment again, or use the 10 landing places you now have to try to predict the next five. As you gather more landing locations, do your predictions become more accurate, less accurate, or similar?

This experiment uses only five past events to predict future events. Scientists use billions of data points to make predictions. They enter the data into complex mathematical models instead of making their own personal predictions. Using more past data and math models increases the accuracy of their predictions, but there will always be factors they cannot account for.

CHAPTER FOUR

CHANGING RAINFALL PATTERNS

Scientists are still learning how shifts in the global climate affect weather patterns. **Meteorologists**, scientists who study the weather, can forecast short-term events.

NEWS

ING NEWS

HURRICANE SLAMS COAST

Meteorologists use tools such as thermometers to measure temperature, barometers to measure air pressure, and anemometers to measure wind speed.

Predicting long-term changes in weather is more difficult, but scientists have learned how temperature changes can lead to larger storms.

Wind turbines capture the energy of wind. Wind is a renewable energy source that does not produce greenhouse gases.

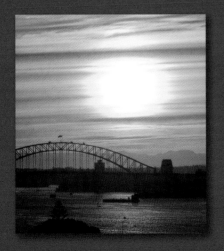

AUSTRALIA'S ANGRY SUMMER

The summer of 2012-2013 was Australia's "Angry Summer," when 123 temperature records broke in three months. The country also reported its hottest day on record, 104.5 degrees Fahrenheit (40.3 degrees Celsius), on January 7, 2013. The government weather agency added a new color, purple, to weather maps to indicate the higher temperatures.

Increased temperatures cause more water to evaporate, and warmer air can hold more water. Each 1 degree Fahrenheit (0.56 degree Celsius) increase in air temperature lets the atmosphere store four percent more water. Storms then have heavier rainfall and a higher chance of flooding.

Not only does flooding destroy homes, businesses, and crops, but it can also spread disease through the water.

One place destroyed by Superstorm Sandy was the famous amusement park at Casino Pier in Seaside Heights, New Jersey.

Scientists worry that bigger changes in the climate will cause stronger storms. Many such events are already occurring. On October 29, 2012, Superstorm Sandy caused flooding along the entire U.S. East Coast, from Maine to Florida. It destroyed nearly 350,000 homes, killed more than 100 people, and caused 65 billion dollars in damage in 24 states.

SPRING TIDES

Regardless of climate change's role in Superstorm Sandy, the full moon made it worse. Spring tides occur during full and new moons. With Earth positioned between the sun and a full moon that October, spring tides were 20 percent higher during the storm. This caused a big storm surge and increased flooding.

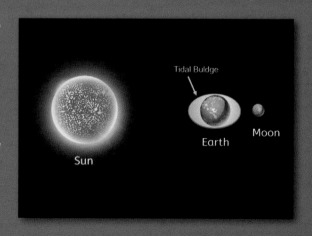

Climate change alone did not cause Superstorm Sandy. But higher sea levels and greater moisture in the air worsened flooding. Warmer seawater also strengthened the storm.

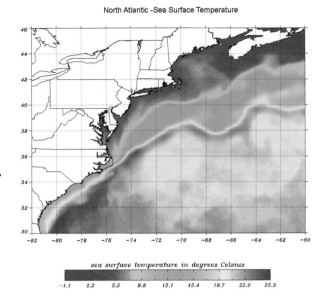

North Atlantic - Sea Surface Temperature

sea surface temperature in degrees Celsius

-1.1 2.2 5.5 8.8 12.1 15.4 18.7 22.0 25.3

Meteorologists can see hurricanes form and move on satellite images. By the time Sandy reached land, it changed from a hurricane to a tropical storm but still caused extensive damage.

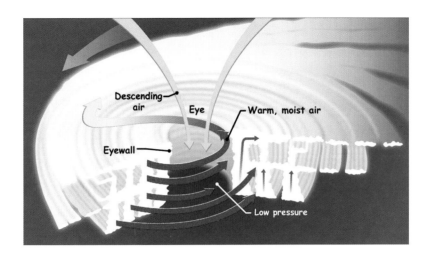

When the moist air above warm water heats and rises, it forms **hurricanes**, violent storms with high winds. With less air with lower pressure at the surface, surrounding high-pressure air fills the gap and rises too. The cycle forms a hurricane, or tropical cyclone. Oceans have grown 1 to 3 degrees Fahrenheit (0.56 to 1.67 degrees Celsius) hotter in the past century. This increase is enough to cause more frequent and severe hurricanes.

Hurricane Wind Scale

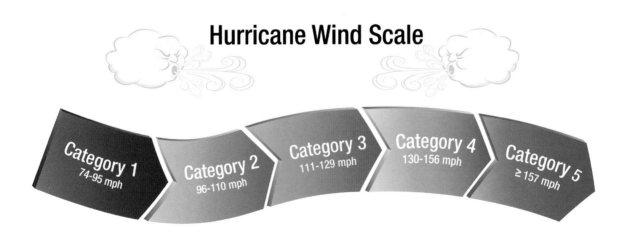

Hurricanes are divided into five categories based on their wind speeds. Lower wind speeds occur in tropical storms or tropical depressions.

Climate skeptics say massive storm cycles occur throughout history and that small climate changes cannot cause big weather changes. True, scientists cannot calculate exactly how much climate change might contribute to a single storm. But they can study storm seasons.

Studying the paths of past hurricanes helps scientists design computer models to try to predict the possible routes of future hurricanes.

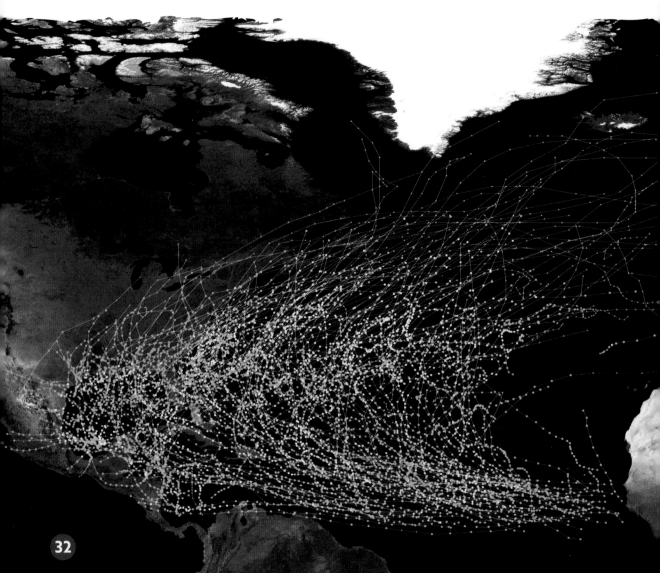

Many scientists worry that severe flooding events will become more common if the climate continues rapidly changing.

The hurricane season of 2017 shows how much climate change might be affecting weather. In under two months, category 4 hurricanes Harvey, Irma, Jose, and Maria hit the U.S. and Caribbean. Harvey, the wettest tropical storm in U.S. history, dropped 33 trillion gallons (125 trillion liters) of water on the Texas coast. Nearly five feet (1.5 meters) of rain flooded Houston and nearby counties.

PUERTO RICO'S DISASTER

Before Houston had time for floodwaters to recede, Hurricane Maria devastated Puerto Rico in the U.S. territory's worst storm in more than 80 years. The entire island lost electricity, and food and clean water became scarce. Even four months later, 1.2 million people, one third of the island's population, lacked power.

CHAPTER FIVE

HEAT WAVES, DROUGHTS, AND WILDFIRES

Changes in climate patterns can also cause too little rainfall. **Droughts** occur when an area does not receive rain for a long time.

Even a few months of drought can destroy a farmer's entire yearly crop if it occurs during key growing seasons.

THE DRIEST DROUGHT

The Eastern Mediterranean experienced the worst drought in 900 years in 1998. Scientists compared tree rings, which show how much water trees received each year, throughout history. They learned Cyprus, Israel, Jordan, Lebanon, Palestine, Syria, and Turkey were 10 to 20 percent drier than the previous nine centuries.

Droughts have disastrous effects on farming, water supply, and wildlife populations. Dry conditions kill crops and damage the soil for years to come. Animals without enough water may migrate away permanently and cause long-term changes to the **ecosystem**, the community of all living organisms in an area.

Droughts also dry out forests and fields. One spark can turn those dry leaves and branches into fuel for devastating wildfires. In 2017, wildfires burned more than 1.5 million acres

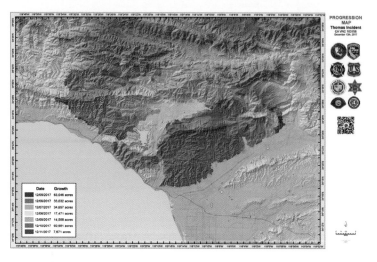

(607,028 hectares) and destroyed over 10,000 homes and buildings in California. Heavy winds and dry conditions made it the most destructive wildfire season in the state's history.

ST. THOMAS'S FIRE

On the evening of December 4, 2017, the largest wildfire in California's history began burning and didn't stop until over a month later. The St. Thomas fire burned through 440 square miles (1,140 square kilometers) before firefighters fully contained it on January 12, 2018.

DIFFERENCES IN EVAPORATION RATES

How quickly does water evaporate in different environments? This activity will help you understand how the surrounding environment affects the speed of evaporation in the same way that different climate conditions can cause water to evaporate more quickly or more slowly.

Evaporation Rate Activity

YOU'LL NEED:

- Five identical disposable bowls (Styrofoam, paper, or plastic)
- Five identical disposable cups
- Water
- Paper
- Pen or pencil
- Marker
- A clock or watch
- ½ cup (120 milliliter) measuring cup

DIRECTIONS:

1. Pick five locations that are very different around your house and yard. Try to find locations that differ in temperature, amount of moisture in the air, and exposure to sunlight. Examples might include a garage, an attic, a bathroom with a shower that's used regularly, the kitchen, the front or back porch (or both), and a window that gets a lot of sunlight.

2. Label one bowl and one cup with each location you choose so that one of each container is assigned to each location.

3. Carefully pour exactly one half cup (120 milliliters) of water into each of the bowls and cups. Repeat steps 2 and 3 four more times.

4. Place one bowl and one cup next to each other in each location. Be sure the containers are out of the way where no one will step on them or knock them over and where no animals will drink from them.

5. Pick a time of day when you can consistently check on the containers. For two weeks, visit each set of containers every two days. Each time, without moving the container of water, use the marker to carefully mark the water level on the inside of each bowl and cup.

6. After two weeks, bring all the cups and bowls together. Compare the changes in water levels. Did the water evaporate at the same rate from a bowl and cup in the same location? Or did the water evaporate faster from one or the other? In which location did water evaporate the fastest? In which did it evaporate the slowest? What factors do you think affected the speed of evaporation in each location?

In a particular geographical area, evaporation levels might be influenced by temperature, humidity (amount of moisture in the air), elevation, time of year, exposure to shade or sunlight, type of soil, the size of puddles or bodies of water, wildlife use of the water, wind patterns, and dozens of other factors.

Increased temperatures also cause heat waves. A 2003 record-breaking **heat wave** in Europe killed tens of thousands of people, and July in 2006 was the warmest month since records began in the United Kingdom, Netherlands, Belgium, Ireland, and Germany.

Difference from average temperature (°F)

RECORD-BREAKING HEATWAVE

One of the biggest heatwaves to hit North America in modern history occurred in 2012. From March 1 to March 27, high temperatures broke more than 7,000 daily record highs, according to the National Oceanic and Atmospheric Administration (NOAA).

More recently, Europeans named the summer heat wave of 2017 "Lucifer." Scientists later determined that climate change made the region's blistering temperatures 10 times more likely.

CHAPTER SIX

SEASONS SHIFTING

The four seasons, spring, summer, autumn, and winter, occur because of Earth's tilt on its axis. When the Northern Hemisphere is tilted toward the sun, it receives more sunlight and heat than the Southern Hemisphere

EARTH'S SEASONS

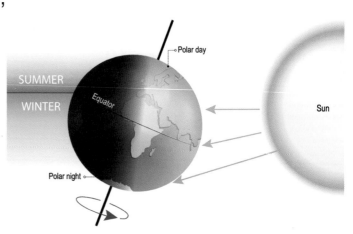

and experiences summer. As the planet continues orbiting the sun, eventually the Southern Hemisphere is tilted toward the sun and has summer while winter descends on the north.

Birds might rely on the weather to know when to migrate.

Seasonal cues, such as snow melting or flowers blooming, affect animal behavior, including mating, migrating, hunting, and hibernating. But climate change is shifting some cues and threatening the stability of ecosystems. Some species are benefiting while others suffer.

SPRINGS STRETCHING OUT

Longer springs and summers can cause health problems for many people. Spring allergy seasons increase for people allergic to pollen and mold, and mosquitos have more time to bite humans and animals. That's especially a problem in regions where mosquitos carry deadly diseases like malaria and dengue fever.

The predator-prey relationship between bobcats and snowshoe hares is an important part of the local ecosystem.

For example, the snowshoe hare turns from brown to white in the winter. Its fur helps it blend into the snow to evade predators. But warmer winters mean less snow. To stay safely camouflaged in winter, these hares are following the snow. In Wisconsin, snowshoe hares have moved about 18 miles (29 kilometers) further north since 1980. But predators like coyotes and bobcats haven't moved with them, so there's less food to go around.

Without snow in the winter, snowshoe hares would be an easy target for predators.

Warmer winters can also cause plants to bloom early—and then die when a frost returns. When birds then migrate to the area to eat plants, the birds don't have enough food either.

HUNGRY, HUNGRY HUMMINGBIRDS

Hummingbirds migrate to the Rocky Mountains in time to drink nectar from blooming flowers each spring. But the flowers are blooming earlier, often before hummingbirds have had a chance to arrive. That means less nectar for the hummingbirds and fewer flowers getting pollinated.

The IPCC has found that spring has arrived two to five days earlier every decade for the past 30 years. Summer arrives 10 days earlier in Europe and six days earlier in China than it did four decades ago. And Chinese winters are now 11 days shorter.

Some animals can keep up with these changes, but others cannot. As climate change throws nature's clock out of sync, scientists are learning as much as they can about what changes will come next.

People who live on small islands worry they will lose everything if sea levels continue rising.

VANISHING ISLANDS

Melting glaciers and sea ice are causing sea levels to rise faster than they have for nearly 3,000 years. Scientists say that human actions have helped oceans increase about 8 inches (20 centimeters) since 1900. Some uninhabited Pacific islands have disappeared, and many island nations are worried they eventually might too.

Glossary

atmosphere (AT-muhs-feer): the mixture of gases that surrounds a planet

climate (KLYE-mit): the weather typical of a place over a long period of time

deforestation (dee-for-ist-STAY-shuhn): to remove or cut down forests

droughts (drouts): long periods without rain that damage crops and cause soil to dry out

ecosystem (EE-koh-sis-tuhm): all the living things in a place and their relation to their environment

fossil fuels (FAH-suhl FYOO-uhls): coal, oil, or natural gas, formed from the remains of prehistoric plants and animals

glaciers (GLAY-shurs): slow-moving masses of ice found in mountain valleys or polar regions

greenhouse gases (GREEN-hous gases): gases such as carbon dioxide and methane that contribute to the greenhouse effect

heat wave (heet wayv): a long period of unusually hot weather

hurricanes (HUR-i-kanes): violent storms with heavy rain and high winds

Index

Show What You Know

1. What is the difference between weather and climate?
2. How can natural events cause climate change?
3. How do humans contribute to climate change?
4. Why is it difficult to accurately predict long-term effects of climate change?
5. What are three possible effects of changing rainfall patterns?

Further Reading

Green, Dan, *Basher Science: Climate Change*, Kingfisher, 2015.

Clinton, Chelsea, *It's Your World: Get Informed, Get Inspired & Get Going!*, Philomel Books, 2015.

Thornhill, Jan, *The Tragic Tale of the Great Auk*, Groundwood Books, 2016.

About the Author

Tara Haelle spent much of her youth exploring creeks and forests outside and reading books inside. Her adventures grew bigger when she became an adult and began traveling across the world to go on exciting adventures such as swimming with sharks, climbing Mt. Kilimanjaro, sailing the Nile, and exploring the Amazon. She earned a photojournalism degree from the University of Texas at Austin so she could keep learning about the world by interviewing scientists and writing about their work. She currently lives in central Illinois with her husband and two sons. You can learn more about her at her website: www.tarahaelle.net.

www.rourkeeducationalmedia.com

PHOTO CREDITS: www.stock.com, www.shutterstock.com, Cover: Sun backround courtesy of NASA, vegetation/drought image courtsey of USGS, ocean Shutterstock by Andrej Filonenko; Pg4; lovemovement, DragonImages, studio023, Pg5; NWS, NOAA. Pg6; ktrifonov, wiratgasem, NOAA. Pg7; Alex_Doubovitsky, Lucy Brown - loca4motion. Pg8;NOAA. Pg9; ablokhin. Pg10; DavidSzabo, ablokhin. Pg11; Alex_Doubovitsky, ginosphotos. Pg12; CreativeNature_nl, rekemp, Noraluca013. Pg13; dutchpilot22, egdigital. Pg14; kotangens, snapgalleria. Pg15; vchal, logoff. Pg16; RTimages. Pg17; disqis, NanoStockk. Pg18; BenGoode, LiliGraphie. Pg19; DavidSzabo, fotojog. Pg20;Casarsa. Pg21; ChiccoDodiFC, AlexanderNikiforov. Pg22; leonello. Pg23; 3000ad, Snowshill. Pg24; chameleonseye, Jevtic, zanskar Pg25; NicoElNino. Pg26; Dmitri Ma, Images_By_Kenny, RugliG, VladisChern. Pg28;mdesigner125, portokalis. Pg29; seclemens, Shutterstock.com, adekvat. Pg30; NASA. Pg31; NASA, Elen11, Images_By_Kenny, John T Takai. Pg32; NOAA, Pg33; Karl Spencer, Mavermick. Pg34; Binty, LofC. Pg35; Taglass, Geerte Verduijn. Pg36;KJimages, JohnCarnemolla. Pg37; valent_ru. Pg38; batuhan toker, VictorHuang. Pg39: SeanPavonePhoto, NOAA, N-sky. Pg40; ttsz, HannamariaH, Widewingsstudio. Pg41; yanikap, mbolina, Wavebreakmedia, TacioPhilip. Pg42; lillitve, Paul Carpenter, twildlife. Pg43; Kristen Howe, billberryphotography, msimpson01. Pg44; Volkovairina, VV-pics, Wanhao Cai PG45; VV-pics

Edited by: Keli Sipperley

Produced by Blue Door Education for Rourke Educational Media. Cover and Interior design by: Jennifer Dydyk

Turning Up the Heat / Tara Haelle
(Taking Earth's Temperature)
  ISBN 978-1-64156-447-2 (hard cover)
  ISBN 978-1-64156-573-8 (soft cover)
  ISBN 978-1-64156-691-9 (e-Book)
Library of Congress Control Number: 2018930474